FASCINATING FACTS & CURIOUS QUESTIONS

This edition printed in 2006 by

CHARTWELL BOOKS, INC.
A Division of BOOK SALES, INC.
114 Northfield Avenue
Edison, New Jersey 08837

Copyright © 2005 Arcturus Publishing Limited
26/27 Bickels Yard, 151–153 Bermondsey Street,
London SE1 3HA

ISBN-13: 978-0-7858-2179-3
ISBN-10: 0-7858-2179-1

Printed in China

CHARTWELL
BOOKS, INC.

Q&A

Life is full of unanswered questions

The purpose of this book is to shed just a little light on some of those perplexing puzzles by using a simple question and answer format, and attempting to tackle some of the queries you always wanted to know the answer to. And even if you've never asked such questions, after reading this book you will be equipped with many fascinating facts with which to entertain your friends and amuse your relatives.

This book is divided into sections, grouping the questions together under the headings: Amazing Animals, Nutty Names & Funny Phrases, Laughable Laws, People & Nature, and Further Funnies.

Amazing Animals covers the curious quirks and features of the various members of the animal kingdom. What colour is a giraffe's tongue? And can they sit down? The answers can be found here, as well as queries about horses, bats, dogs and sheep – and many more. Nutty Names & Funny Phrases tells you why certain unusual expressions have become popular and where they originated from.

Laughable Laws looks at the strange laws from around the world, and examines why they came into being. The natural world and the human body are the main subjects in Nature & People, which also looks at individual achievements. Further Funnies discusses anything and everything that was not mentioned in the earlier chapters.

Freaky, funny and fascinating – all of these facts have to be read to be believed.

Q

Amazing Animals

The animal kingdom is full of fascinating creatures with all kinds of strange abilities and physical features. But are things really as they appear? In the following section, you will find out why zebras have stripes, why elephants can't jump, and whether bats really are blind. Discover how many legs a centipede has and whether penguins have knees. Some of the answers may surprise you, or teach you something about our furry or feathered friends that you didn't know. Or they might just give you a good giggle...

 Why is a dog's nose wet?

 Dogs don't always have wet noses. Many very healthy dogs have dry noses at least part of the time. The simple explanation is that most dogs tend to lick their noses often and this is why they are usually wet.

 Why does the stork carry babies?

 The winsome image of a stork winging towards a thankful couple, a baby in a bundle hanging from its beak comes from Europe, where people noticed that in some areas, the number of storks roosting and the number of human babies born seemed to be related. From this, people made the link between storks and the birth of babies. Storks are also extremely maternal creatures, so this may also have contributed to the myth.

 Why can't a horse be sick?

 Horses have a band of muscle around the oesophagus as it enters the stomach. This band operates in horses much as in humans: as a one-way valve. Food freely passes down the oesophagus into the stomach as the valve relaxes, but the valve squeezes down the opening and cuts off the passage for food going back up.

Horses, however, differ from us because their valve really works. Humans can vomit. Horses almost physically can't because of the power of that cut-off valve muscle. Also, the oesophagus meets the stomach at an angle which enhances the cut-off function when the horse's stomach is bloated with food or gas. Then the stomach wall pushes against the valve, closing off the oesophagus even more completely from the stomach. Normally, the mechanics are such that the horse's stomach ruptures before the valve yields.

Q Are bats really blind?

A In short, no. Many bats see very well and most fruit-eating bats locate their food by sight. However, the phrase 'blind as a bat' came about because some bats rely on their other senses when hunting for food (usually insects) in the dark. They do this by sending out streams of high-pitched noise from their mouth or nose. When this sound bounces off objects and sends back echoes, the bat can use its amazing ears to determine the location, size, distance and shape of an object. These sounds are too high-pitched for humans to hear, but they can tell a bat whether the nearby insect is an edible one or not! So, bats are not blind, they just do not rely on their sight.

Q Why don't sheep shrink in the rain?

A Because they all already have! Actually, the process of shrinking wool, known as 'felting' requires warm water, heat, and also friction – the latter two are usually absent from even the heaviest of rainstorms.

Q **Why can't elephants jump?**

A Although elephants have the same number of bones in their feet as other mammals, the bones are more tightly packed together in an elephant's foot, therefore the flexibility or spring mechanisms are not there. Not to mention the sheer amount of weight that they would be attempting to get off the ground!

Q **What is the biggest killer in the insect world?**

A Surprisingly, it has to be the humble mosquito, responsible for infecting humans with such diseases as encephalitis, malaria and Dengue fever. The World Health Organisation estimates that mosquitoes are responsible for more than two million deaths per year – so here are a few tips on avoiding them: Wear mosquito repellent. Although mosquito repellents do not actually repel mosquitoes, what they do is 'hide' you by blocking the mosquitoes' sensors so they don't know you are there. Also, cut down on bananas, as research shows you are more likely to be a target for mosquitoes if you eat bananas.

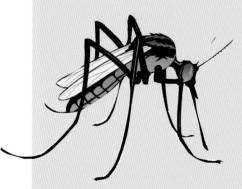

Other deadly bugs include the humble honeybee – which kills more people annually than all the poisonous snakes in the world combined – and the tsetse fly, which kills another 66,000 a year.

Q How do French poodles get their distinctive style?

A Believe it or not, the puffy-tailed, be-ribboned classic show-dog style originated when the poodle was used across Europe as a hunting dog. Their thick coats proved to be a hindrance when it came to navigating the thick undergrowth and swimming, so the hunters shaved their dogs hindquarters – leaving the distinctive cuffs around the ankles and hips to protect against rheumatism. They would also mark out their dogs with a particular ribbon, so each hunter could tell which dogs belonged to him. And so from these unlikely roots sprang the show-dog.

Q Are pigs really dirty?

A Although they have a mucky image, pigs actually keep themselves cleaner than many household pets. The reason they lie in the mud is because they have no sweat glands, and therefore cannot cool themselves down. Pigs are rated the fourth most intelligent animal on the planet and can be found on every continent except Antarctica. There are over 180 species of pig, they have an average life span of 20 years, and litters of between two and 12 piglets. In the olden days, sea captains would always carry a pig aboard their ship as – in the case of being shipwrecked – it was thought that pigs would swim towards the nearest shore.

How many legs do millipedes and centipedes have?

 The literal translation of the words 'centipede' and 'millipede' means one hundred and one thousand legs respectively, which is certainly not the case. Depending on the species, a centipede will have anything between 10 and 100 legs, while the maximum amount for a millipede is 400. The way to tell the difference between the two is, centipedes have one pair of legs on each of their body segments, while millipedes have two pairs per segment – except for the first three segments, which have one pair each.

Q How long is a giraffe's tongue?

A Giraffes' tongues can reach anywhere up to 50cm! This is used to help them get leaves from further back on the branch, as they obviously have no hands or paws to hold the branches with. Another unusual thing about a giraffe's tongue is that it is blue-black in colour. Although no one is sure about why this is, it has been suggested that it is to protect their tongue from getting sunburnt!

Q Can giraffes sit down?

A According to the Kruger National Park, giraffes can in fact sit down, but rarely do, preferring to sleep standing up, in much the same way as horses.

Q Do penguins have knees?

A Yes. Penguins appear to have very short legs and no knees because only the lower leg is externally visible. Their knees and upper legs are feather covered, hiding them from view. This also means that penguins never get cold knees!

Q Why do zebras have stripes?

A Believe it or not, it is to camouflage them and keep them safe from one certain predator. Animals that inhabit areas with tall grass often have long, vertical stripes. The nature of these stripes means the individual zebra can hide in areas of long grass and escape detection by a lion. This works because lions are colour-blind and therefore cannot see the difference between the zebra and the grass. The stripes can also serve as a visual disruption, as they are positioned so that they seem to be a separate design superimposed on top of the animal.

This makes it hard for the predator to get a clear sense of where the animal begins and ends – the pattern on the body seems to run off in every direction. Also, to a lion, a group of zebras would all blur together and not stand out as individuals, making it hard for the lion to attack one specific zebra.

Q Are lovebirds affectionate?

A They are indeed. The affection that they show for each other is how they got their name. Also, lovebirds will often pair up and stay together for life. They will stay physically very close, and often groom each other.

Lovebirds are small parrots, and have been kept as pets for more than 100 years. There are nine different species, within which a large range of colours have been bred and developed.

Q How does a chameleon change colour?

A It is a misconception that chameleons change colour to match their environment. This is not the case – their change in colour is brought about by a combination of temperature, light, and the emotional state of the chameleon itself. What created this misconception is that chameleons mainly alternate between the colours of green, brown and grey, which are usually the colour of their background. The key to a chameleon's ability to change colour is the cell layers beneath its transparent skin. Some of these layers contain pigments, while others reflect light to create new colours.

Q How many minks does it take to make a coat?

A The horrible fact is that anywhere between 35 and 65 minks must die in order to make just one mink fur coat. Other creatures that are forced to die for human fashion are beavers (15 make one coat), fox (between 15 and 25), chinchilla (60 to 100), and ermine (150).

Q Do lemmings really commit mass suicide?

A In a word, no. Although it is a common belief that lemmings queue up to jump off cliffs, it is, quite simply, not true. A 1958 documentary called *White Wilderness* appeared to show this happening, but the shots were set up by the director. Occasionally, when population growth is too high, some lemmings will migrate to a less populated area. When this happens, some lemmings die due to an unfamiliarity with their new environment. However, when there is competition for space or mates, lemmings are more likely to fight and kill each other than kill themselves.

Q What creature has the biggest brain?

A A tough question, as the answer depends on context. While an elephant's brain weighs 5,000g and a blue whale's doubles that at a whopping 10,000g, when taken in proportion with the rest of the body, the whale's brain is smaller than man's. It was assumed that this was the reason for man's superiority over the other creatures, until it was discovered that – while man has 1g of brain for every 44g of body – the dwarf monkey has 1g of brain for every 27g of body, and the capuchin monkey has 1g of brain for every 17.5g of body.

Q What is the loudest animal?

A The blue whale – as well as being enormous, with a massive brain – is also the loudest creature in the world, with a call that can level up to a staggering 188 decibels and be heard for hundreds of miles under water. To give you some perspective, a jet engine taking off is about 150 decibels, and a rocket launching is about 180. The second loudest creature is the howler monkey.

Q Can an albatross really sleep while it flies?

A Indeed it can, and what is really scary is the fact that the big birds apparently choose to grab forty winks while cruising along at about 25mph!

Q What is the fastest swimmer in the ocean?

A Reaching a speed of 68mph, the Sailfish wins, although strictly speaking this is their 'leaping', rather than 'swimming', speed. Coming in last place would be the Sea Horse, which ambles along at a steady 0.01mph. Dolphins manage a respectable 25mph, while sharks can chase their prey at an impressive 44mph. To give you some perspective, human beings can run at about 21mph.

Q Why is there only one queen bee per hive?

A A queen bee will lay several fertilised eggs to develop into queen bees. However, it is something of a race to be born first, as the first queen bee out of the egg will quickly kill all the other unborn queens and rule the hive alone.

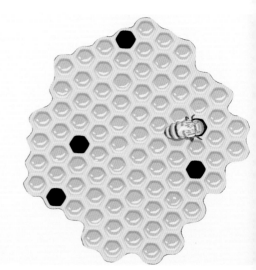

How many species of animals are there?

A Over one million. This includes 73,000 different kinds of spider, 6,000 species of reptile, and 3,000 types of lice. And the 4,600 different kinds of mammal make up just 0.3% of animals, while birds cover only 0.7%. To give you a clue where the rest of the numbers come from, scientists have identified over 920,000 different species of insect, with another 2,000 being discovered and named every year.

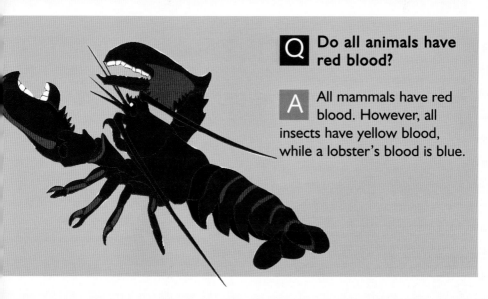

Q **Do all animals have red blood?**

A All mammals have red blood. However, all insects have yellow blood, while a lobster's blood is blue.

Q Why are some hens' eggs brown and some white?

A Believe it or not, white eggs come from hens with white feathers and brown eggs come from hens with red feathers. Although the different colour eggs are produced by different breeds of hen, there is no difference in flavour or nutrients. Hens produce one egg every 24-26 hours, after which they take half an hour's break before starting again. Some hens also take a day off every 3-5 days, while the workaholic hens only rest every 10 days.

Q How do Emperor penguins protect their eggs?

A In this branch of the animal kingdom, it is the males that look after their unborn offspring. The loving father will keep his eggs on his feet, covered with a feathered flap of tummy. He will brace the bitter Antarctic cold for the 60 days or more that it takes for the eggs to hatch – and they do not eat a thing for the entire time they are doing this. When their babies hatch, the father feeds the chick a special liquid from the back of his throat. Then, when the mother penguin returns, the father goes out to the sea for a well-earned rest.

Q What birds lay the largest and smallest eggs?

A The largest egg is that of the ostrich, which is about 18cm long, 14cm wide and weighs about 12kg. This is about 2,000 times larger than the smallest bird's egg, which is produced by the humming-bird. Hummingbird eggs are 1.2cm long, 0.8cm wide and weigh less than 0.2g.

Q

Nutty Names & Funny Phrases

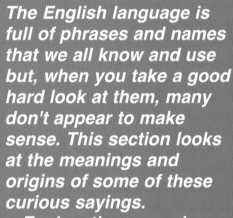

The English language is full of phrases and names that we all know and use but, when you take a good hard look at them, many don't appear to make sense. This section looks at the meanings and origins of some of these curious sayings.

Explanations are given for phrases and words such as 'goody two-shoes', 'on the wagon', 'honeymoon' and 'blue-blooded'. Also, you'll find out the origins of some well-known nursery rhymes and why we refer to New York as the 'The Big Apple' and its Stock Exchange as 'Wall Street'.

Q Why do they say 'a cat has got your tongue'?

A An animal that pops up in many unusual phrases, the cat is said to have nine lives due to its careful and suspicious nature, plus its ability to land on its feet after a long fall. The 'nine lives' saying goes back to before the 16th century and is probably the reason for the naming of the cat-o'-nine-tails. It is thought that when the use of this cruel device became well known, the threat of a beating from it would often render the proposed victim mute. It was then asked of the poor soul, 'cat got your tongue?' And while on the subject of cats appearing in phrases, 'the cat's pyjamas' is said to have come from an English tailor, EB Katz, of the 1700s who advertised his product – luxury silk pyjamas – with the slogan, 'Nothing like a cat nap in Katz pyjamas'.

Q Why is New York City called The Big Apple?

A First used in *The Wayfarer*, a 1909 book edited by Edward S Martin, the metaphor read as follows: 'New York was merely one of the fruits of that great tree whose roots go down in the Mississippi Valley, and whose branches spread from one ocean to the other... [But] the big apple [New York] gets a disproportionate share of the national sap.' This phrase was brought to more prominence in the 1920s when sports writer for the *New York Morning Telegraph*, John J Fitzgerald called his racing column 'Around the Big Apple' after hearing stable hands on the racing scene use the phrase to describe the city. In the 18 February, 1924 column he wrote: 'The Big Apple. The dream of every lad that ever threw a leg over a thoroughbred and the goal of all horsemen. There's only one Big Apple. That's New York.'

Q Why is Bob your uncle?

A The phrase 'Bob's your uncle', meaning a sure thing or something happening fast, probably comes from an event of nepotism in 1887, when Lord Salisbury – known to his friends as Robert or Bob – appointed his nephew to the position of Chief Secretary for Ireland. The implication being that, if Bob's your uncle, things will happen quickly and the outcome is sure to be favourable!

Q What is a red-letter day?

A The phrase 'a red letter day' was originated from the First Book of Common Prayer, 1549, in which every Sunday was marked in red, as well as every Christian festival (such as Easter and Christmas) and the Saints' days. The phrase was adopted into the language to mean any special occasion or memorable day.

Q Where does the name Teddy Bear originate?

A A nice story has it that US President Theodore 'Teddy' Roosevelt was on a hunting trip in Mississippi in 1902, but was having no luck as the local game seemed to be in hiding. One of his aides then captured a bear cub and offered it to the President to kill. Roosevelt declared that this would be unsporting and freed the cub. When this incident was caricatured in the *Washington Post*, the cartoon was seen by sweet shop owner Morris Michtom. He asked his wife to make a toy 'Teddy's bear' to display in their New York shop window, alongside the cartoon. The stuffed bear proved such a hit that within a year, the Michtoms were out of the sweet shop business and had created the Ideal Novelty and Toy Company, which is still a successful company today.

Q Why do people say 'the cat's out of the bag' when a secret is revealed?

A This saying dates back to the shady marketplace dealings of Medieval England. Pigs were commonly bought and sold at the marketplace, and they would often be placed in a bag or sack, so the buyer could easily transport their precious purchase home. However, some traders were less than honest, and would replace the valuable pigs with large – but inexpensive and common – cats. When the cats escaped, or a canny buyer demanded to see the contents of the sack, then the cat was out of the bag – the game was up. This practice is also where the phrase 'pig in a poke' (meaning buying an unknown) originates as the sacks were also known as pokes.

Q What do the 'p' and 'q' stand for in the phrase 'mind your p's and q's'?

A Although this phrase has been in use since the late 18th century, there is some debate over what the letters stand for. Some believe that the phrase created by teachers telling their pupils to be careful, so as to avoid confusing the two letters when learning to write and spell. This may have led to the phrase being taken to mean 'be careful' or 'take care'. Another similar theory regards typesetters for books and newspapers, who used to load the letters backwards and would, therefore, run the risk of mixing up the two letters 'p' and 'q'.

A different theory comes from the pubs of England, where it used to be the custom for the landlord to keep a note of a customer's tab on a blackboard behind the bar. This system used the abbreviations 'p' for pints and 'q' for quarts. Customers were advised to 'mind their p's and q's' to ensure they were not overcharged by an unscrupulous landlord.

The phrase now is taken to mean 'mind your manners', while some think the phrase stands for 'mind your problems and questions', which fits well with the modern meaning of the phrase.

Q Where did the term 'swashbuckler' originate?

A Most commonly used to describe such film heroes such as Errol Flynn and Douglas Fairbanks, the word is often misunderstood, and people talk about Flynn 'buckling his swash'. Although this sounds funny, the correct phrase would be 'swashes his buckler'. A buckler was a small shield. The word 'swash' is thought to have come from the sound a sword makes when it clashes against a shield, and initially someone 'swashing' was dashing about, waving a sword while just pretending to fight. Originally a swashbuckler was not a flattering term, referring to a man who made a lot of show, but did not really like to fight. A writer in 1560 described a man as 'a drunkard, a gambler and a swashbuckler'. When the silent movie star Douglas Fairbanks dashed around on screen waving his sword around but only pretending to fight, the word was reborn as a flattering description of a handsome movie hero.

Q Why do we call well-behaved people 'goody two-shoes'?

A The phrase 'goody two-shoes' is usually applied to someone who may be technically behaving impeccably, but is doing so in a sickening or smug manner, and is more insulting than complimentary. The name originates from a nursery story, thought to have been written by Oliver Goldsmith and published in 1765, entitled *The History of Goody Two Shoes*. The main character of the story was called Margery Meanwell and she had only one shoe. When she found the other, she was so smug and pleased with herself that she went round telling everyone that she had 'two shoes'. The name Goody was a common name for married women, as it was an abbreviation of the term 'goodwife'. From this tale came the nickname for someone who is acting in a self-righteous or smug manner.

Q **What does OK stand for?**

A The origin of OK has been debated for a long time. What is in no doubt is that it appeared in print in *The Boston Morning Post* in 1839 and was taken to mean 'all correct'. Some suggestions of what the letters stand for are as follows: The abbreviation of Orrin Kendall biscuits, which soldiers ate during the American Civil War; the initials of Old Keokuk, a Native American who signed treaties with his initials; short for Aux Cayes, a Haitian port that American sailors praised for its rum; or a version of the Choctaw 'okeh', which means 'indeed'. What cannot be disputed is that the popularity of OK runs parallel with the global spread of American culture.

Q **What do the birds and the bees have to do with reproduction?**

A About as much as any other animal. This reference – often more confusing than enlightening – dates from days when sex education contained the odd reference to birds laying eggs and bees pollinating flowers. Inspiration may have come from Samuel Coleridge's words: 'All nature seems at work... The bees are stirring, birds are on the wing./And I the while, the sole unbusy thing,/Not honey make, nor pair, nor build, nor sing.'

Q **Why is losing your job known as being fired?**

A Originally known as being 'fired out', it is thought this term comes from the phrase used in discharging a firearm, therefore meaning that the person has been ejected from the company. However, there is also a theory that it refers to an old clan practice of burning the houses of unwanted clansmen.

Q Do bees have knees?

A They do indeed! In fact, a bee's pollen baskets, or corbiculae, are located on the midsections of its legs. However, why people refer to something excellent as 'the bee's knees' is not as clear-cut. It has been suggested that 'bee's knees' could be a reference to the pollen baskets, therefore the concentrated goodness to be found there. Some believe it is a development of 'b's and 'e's, short for be-alls and end-alls. However, the general agreement is that 'bee's knees' has lasted so long simply because it rhymes, as opposed to other sayings, such as 'the flea's eyebrows', 'the canary's tusks' and 'the clam's garter'.

Q Can it really rain cats and dogs?

A The simple answer to this question is no, it cannot. So why do people say it? Many suggestions have been offered, ranging from cats falling off roofs during storms to the rare French word *catadoupe*, meaning waterfall. However, there are other similes that have been used in the past that depict it as the falling of unlikely objects – such as pitchforks, hammer handles and chicken coops – as a way of describing the noise and confusion of a storm, and it is likely that this is where the phrase originated. So, it may not rain cats and dogs – but how about fish and frogs? That has actually happened – although not both at the same time! Fish fell from the skies in London in 1984 and Great Yarmouth in 2000, and in 1844, again in England, frogs fell from the clouds. This is possible because powerful updrafts created during thunderstorms form mini tornados, which can suck up things in their path – such as fish or frogs swimming close to the surface if the storm brews at sea or over a river.

Q Where does the phrase 'flipping the bird' come from?

A Meaning to dismiss someone, to flip the bird is a description of a rude hand gesture designed to offend the person you are dismissing. The phrase – before being tied to the hand gesture – came from Australian theatre of the 1880s. There, to give an actor the 'bird' was to hiss him off the stage, the 'bird' in question being a goose. The term came to mean to treat someone with derision in the hope of dismissing them, although it is unclear exactly when and why it became coupled to the hand gesture.

Q Where did the word 'honeymoon' originate?

A It is popularly thought that the wedding practices of Ancient Babylon, 4,000 years ago, led to this word. Apparently, it was the custom then for the father of the bride to provide the bridegroom with all the mead he could drink for a calendar month after the wedding. As mead is a honey beer, so the period after the wedding became known as the 'honey month'. The story goes that somewhere along the way – possibly because the calendar of Ancient Babylon was a lunar one – 'honey month' became the more familiar 'honeymoon'. However, the real origin is not so romantic. It first appeared in the English language in the 16th century and referred to the period after marriage when all was as sweet as honey, but, like the moon, this charmed period soon wanes.

Q Why are people who are the centre of attention said to be 'in the limelight'?

A Lighthouses used to burn lime before electricity was invented, as it gave off a very bright light. After some time, this practice spread to the theatre, where lime was burned to create a spotlight effect, singling out the lead character on the stage. That person, who was the centre of everyone's attention, was then said to be in the limelight.

Q **Why is the site of a disaster described as 'Ground Zero'?**

A Now most often associated with the 9/11 World Trade Center atrocity in New York, the phrase originated in 1946 and referred to the disaster sites that were left when the atom bombs were dropped on Hiroshima and Nagasaki. In these instances, Ground Zero was the place on the ground closest to where the blast took place, and all distances from the blast were measured in a radius from that point. After a couple of decades the phrase began to develop to mean the centre of something, for example 'Paris is the ground zero of fashion this year'. Now – after 9/11 – it has gone back to its darker original meaning.

Q **Why do people say 'going to hell in a handbasket'?**

A The phrase, meaning to deteriorate quickly, seems to have originated in America in the early 1900s, although it doesn't appear in print until the Fifties. A handbasket was a woven basket (with a handle) that was light and floated easily. The phrase came about as something deteriorating would be said to be going to hell, meaning going downhill. The addition of 'in a handbasket' indicates the quick progression of the descent.

Q Was there really an Old King Cole?

A The nursery rhyme would have us believe that Old King Cole was a 'merry old soul' and, while that cannot be verified, it is believed that there was a King Cole who ruled in Britain in the 3rd century AD. His existence was later recorded by 12th century chronicler Geoffrey of Monmouth. Cole is said to have built Colchester, and there is still a Roman gravel pit there, called King Cole's Kitchen.

Whether Cole really ever called for his 'fiddlers three' will never be known, although Geoffrey of Monmouth mentions that Cole's daughter was a talented musician.

Q Why do we refer to a 'Mexican wave'?

A A Mexican wave refers to the action of a large group of people, usually in a sporting arena, standing up in turn and raising their hands in the air before sitting down again, creating a ripple or wave effect. Although the practice may have originated elsewhere, the Mexican wave became so-called when it was televised to an international audience of millions during the 1986 World Cup, held in Mexico City.

Q Where does the phrase 'paint the town red' originate?

A The first people to 'paint the town red' were either the Native Americans or the cowboys they fought with – however, back then the phrase meant something quite different. A town that had been 'painted red' was one that had been burnt down, the 'red' referring to the colour of the flames, or had suffered heavy casualties, with the 'red' referring to the blood spilt. The phrase then meant to destroy a town, and was used when drunken cowboys would shoot up towns while 'enjoying' themselves. This led to the phrase's meaning today, to go out and have a good – if slightly wild – time.

Q Where does the phrase 'wet your whistle' come from?

A The often repeated myth is that in English pubs, regulars would often have a whistle baked into the side, rim or handle of their ceramic cups that they drank their ale out of. When they wanted a refill, they would blow on the whistle to get the barmaid's attention. This practice apparently led to the phrase 'wet your whistle', indicating getting a drink. However, the phrase doesn't refer to an actual whistle. A 'whistle' was a slang word for a mouth or throat, especially in regard to speaking or singing, and it is easier to whistle if your lips are wet. So, 'wet your whistle' is just a way of making having a drink sound like a necessity.

Q Why are policemen referred to as bobbies or cops?

A This nickname originated in 1828, when the Metropolitan Police Act was passed in London, creating the modern police force and putting an end to the vigilante justice that had gone before. The Home Secretary at that time was Sir Robert Peel, and therefore policemen were nicknamed 'bobbies', 'Roberts' or 'peelers'. Although 'peelers' is still used in some areas of Ireland, 'Roberts' never really caught on. 'Cops' is an abbreviation of the nickname 'coppers', the origin of which has been debated – some believe it comes from the copper buttons on a London officer's uniform, or the copper badge worn by the very first New York policemen. However, it is more likely that 'cop', meaning to capture, came into the language as an abbreviation of the Latin word meaning to capture, *capere*. The first instance of 'copper' in print, referring to a policeman, was in 1846. It had been shortened to 'cop' by 1859.

Q Why do people say 'goodnight, sleep tight'?

A This phrase originates from around the time of William Shakespeare. Obviously this was way before the sprung mattresses of today came into being, and so mattresses were secured to the bed frame by ropes. You would pull the ropes tight to make the bed firmer to sleep on, and therefore more comfortable. The ropes would sometimes come loose during the night, so it was considered a good night's sleep if the bed stayed tight.

Q Why is someone said to be 'blue-blooded'?

A The phrase is thought to have originated in Spain as an expression to show the difference between the aristocracy from those with Jewish or African ancestry. For those with very pale complexions, their veins appeared blue through their skin. This continued into Victorian times, when the rich were always very pale as a suntan was considered evidence that you were poor and had to work outside doing hard manual labour to earn a living, while pale skin showed that you had enough money to stay indoors and not work.

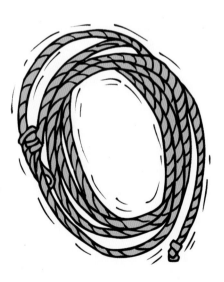

Q Why is someone said to be living 'the life of Reilly'?

A This phrase was first used in a song in 1919 in the lyric 'but I'm living the life of Reilly just the same'. Then, as now, the phrase meant to be living a good life with plenty of material goods and great fortune. It is believed that the origin of this phrase is another song, this time called *Is That Really Mr Reilly?* This song was first performed in the 1880s and contained such lyrics as 'a hundred a day would be my pay'. The subject of the song was comedic speculation as to what 'Mr Reilly' would do if he became a rich man.

Q Where does the term 'big cheese' come from?

A Meaning someone who is well known and important in their field, 'big cheese' was developed over several years, beginning in London in the early 19th century. However, the phrase had nothing to do with cheese as it originally stemmed from the Persian or Hindi word *chiz* meaning 'thing'. Anglo-Indians would often call something 'the real chiz', combining English and their native language. However, when English people heard the unfamiliar word, they converted it into something they understood – even if the phrase no longer made much sense. This led to the development of the phrase 'big cheese' in America in the early 20th century, where it was one of several 'big' descriptions, such as 'big shot' and 'big banana', which all probably stemmed from the British phrase 'bigwig'. 'Bigwig' came from the practice of the privileged classes wearing large powdered wigs in the 18th century.

Q Why is someone who is being ignored said to be 'sent to Coventry'?

A The phrase first appeared in print in 1647, in *The History of Rebellion and Civil Wars in England*, written by the First Earl of Clarendon, Edward Hyde. However, the phrase is used quite literally, referring to Royalist troops being captured during the English Civil Wars of the 1640s and taken to Coventry for security, where they were not made welcome. Another explanation is that, around the same time, the people of Coventry disapproved so strongly of the soldiers who were billeted there that they refused to speak to them. The soldiers then passed along the phrase as a way of saying that someone was being given the silent treatment.

Q Was there a Doctor Foster, like in the nursery rhyme?

A There was indeed – however, it is believed that Doctor Foster is in fact a code name for none other than England's King Edward I. The rhyme was inspired by the monarch's trip to Gloucester during a shower of rain. However, the King did not 'step in a puddle right up to his middle', although the streets were flooded. Planks were laid down for the king's horse to walk on to avoid sinking in to the mud, but the damage was done and the ruler's overall impression of the town was so bad that he swore never to return. So the locals made up a rhyme about a man who visited Gloucester, and then 'never went there again'. Why they chose 'Doctor Foster' we will never know, apart from the fact that it rhymes with Gloucester.

Q Why is swearing off alcohol known as being 'on the wagon'?

A This is an American expression, dating back to before the roads were paved. To avoid large chocking dust clouds, a horse-drawn water carriage would spray the streets and dampen down the dust. If someone had sworn off alcohol, they were said to be climbing aboard the water wagon, which was shortened over time to 'on the wagon'.

Q Why is being in suspense referred to as 'being on tenterhooks'?

A The phrase was first used – according to the Oxford English Dictionary – by Tobias Smollet in the mid-18th century, when he wrote: 'I left him upon the tenterhooks of impatient uncertainty.' Back then, most people would have known what tenterhooks were – a tenter derived its name from the Latin word *tendere*, meaning to stretch, and that is exactly what they did. A tenter was a wooden frame, on which wet cloth was hung to stretch and dry. The tenterhooks were attached to the frame, from which the cloth would hang. Armed with this information, it is easy to see why something in a painful state of suspense could be said to be on tenterhooks.

Q Is the nursery rhyme 'Ring a Ring o' Roses' really about the Bubonic Plague?

A The story that the children's rhyme originates from the time of the Black Death is morbid, but is almost certainly correct. Each seemingly cheerful lyric reflects a stage of the disease. The 'ring o' roses' refers to the rash sported by sufferers shortly after contracting the disease, while 'a pocketful of posies' was either thought to ward off the plague, or else it covered the smell of the dead and dying. The sneezing represents the final days of the sufferer, until 'we all fall down'. However, the earliest recorded references to 'Ring around the Rosie' are as recent as the mid-19th century, and no clear explanation has been found for the various versions of the rhyme.

Q Why are some people described as 'straight-laced'?

A In the olden days, ladies of high society would wear corsets pulled in tight to make their waists smaller. However, when wearing these corsets, the women could not do very much as their movement and even breathing were very restricted. The phrase 'straight-laced' was inspired by the straight lacing of the corset and came to mean someone who was very proper – as these ladies were – but who could not really let loose and have a good time.

Q What are the origins of the phrase 'scot-free'?

A When someone has got away with something scot-free, it usually means without responsibility, consequences or blame. The phrase, however, has nothing to do with the Scottish. Rather the word 'scot' here refers to an old English word meaning 'payment' in relation to a tab run up at a tavern or an entertainment expense. The phrase therefore originally meant 'to get away without paying money' and has, over time, become just 'to get away without paying' in any way. The phrase has been developing since it was first used in the 16th century.

Q Why do people say
'in my neck of the woods'?

A When America was first settled, people wanted to find new
names for places rather than using the traditional English names
such as 'moor', 'heath', 'dell' and 'fen'. They came up with 'branch',
'fork', 'hollow' and 'neck'. 'Neck' had been used in England to mean
an area of land in a narrow strip. However,
the settlers were the first to apply it to a
narrow strip of woodland. When
houses were built there, 'my neck of
the woods' suddenly came to mean
'my home area', and that was how
the phrase was passed down.

Q Why are frankfurter sausages also called hot dogs?

A Originally, the Austrian wiener sausages were nicknamed by a
butcher the 'dachshund sausage' after his pet dog, whose long
thin body they resembled. The name stuck, and the sausages proved
very popular. In 1871, the first stand selling the sausages was set up on
Coney Island, New York, by German butcher Charles Feltman. He
wrapped the sausages in a milk bread roll. However, the snack was
not known as a hot dog until 1901 when a cartoonist Tad Dorgan saw
a vendor use the bread roll to handle the sausage after burning his
fingers. The situation struck him as amusing, and he decided to make it
into a comic strip. The only problem was, he couldn't spell dachshund,
and so called the
snack 'hot dog
sausages' instead.
Unfortunately the
original cartoon has
never been found to
support this story.

Q What does 'to the bitter end' mean?

A Now taken to mean staying on to the last minute no matter what happens, the phrase is thought to be a nautical expression referring to the end of a cable attached to a 'bit'. *The Oxford English Dictionary* explains: 'A ship is "brought up to a bitter" when the cable is allowed to run out to that stop. When a chain or rope is paid out to the bitter-end, no more remains to let go.'

Q How did Wall Street get its name?

A When pigs used to run wild on Manhattan Island, the residents built a long wall on the northern edge of what is now Lower Manhattan to stop the pigs from running through their grain fields. The street that ran alongside the wall was Wall Street.

Q Who is Melba Toast named after?

A The same person that Peach Melba is. Dame Nellie Melba, the Australian opera singer, was the inspiration behind both dishes, as both were favourites of the star. Peach Melba was created for her by Auguste Escoffier when she stayed at the Savoy in 1893.

Q Why are English sailors known as 'limeys'?

A Scurvy was once the scourge of the ocean, killing many sailors. Captain Cook lost 41 of his 98-man crew on his first voyage to the South Pacific in 1768. However, it was discovered that citrus juice would prevent the disease, so British ships began travelling with a large supply of limes and lime juice, much to the amusement of other nations' fleets who came up with the nickname. However, it could have been worse – by 1795 lemon juice was standard issue on all British navy ships. Yes, they could have ended up being called lemons instead!

Q Why were British soldiers known as 'Tommies' in the Second World War?

A When they enlisted, British soldiers had to fill in a form. On the form were example answers to help them fill it in correctly. The sample name on the form was Thomas Atkins. It was fortunate for the Americans that they didn't get their nickname in the same way – the sample name on their forms was John Smith.

Q Where did the word 'malaria' originate?

A How this fatal disease was spread was not known when it was named. Originally, people thought that it was carried on the air, and so the name 'malaria' was made from the Latin words, *mal* and *aria*, meaning 'bad air'.

In actual fact, the disease is carried via water and not air.

Q Where did the term 'encyclopaedia' come from?

A The word 'encyclopaedia' is an amalgamation of two Greek words which mean 'circle of learning'. The oldest encyclopaedia was written in Greece over 2,000 years ago. The oldest encyclopaedia that still exists was written by the Roman scholar Pliny the Elder in the 1st century AD. The first volume of the *Encyclopaedia Britannica* was published in 1771.

Q Why do people say 'it'll cost you an arm and a leg'?

A The story often given is that back in the days before photography was invented, people would often pay to sit in front of a painter for a formal portrait. Often the price of the picture would depend not on how many people were painted, but how many limbs were in the picture, as the detailing of them would cost more. Therefore the phrase, 'it'll cost you an arm and a leg' came to stand for costing someone a high price. However, this has no basis in fact. The earliest recorded use of the phrase dates back only to 1956. Billie Holliday, in her autobiography *Lady Sings the Blues*, writes: 'Finally she found someone who sold her some stuff for an arm and a leg.' Almost certainly, she did not coin the phrase – it might just be an extension of the older phrase 'I'd give my right arm for', which indicates that the speaker would be willing to make a great sacrifice to obtain or do something.

Q Laughable Laws

Although laws are meant to have been made for our protection, some of them seem as though they were solely designed to make us laugh. Here is a collection of some of the more silly and meaningless laws from around the world, each with an explanation as to how they came into being. Some laws are old, a few make sense with a good explanation... but many just suffer from not being thought through properly. In this section, find out why you cannot step on the currency in Thailand; where in America high-heeled shoes are banned; why it is illegal to get drunk in a pub in the UK; and why chewing gum is against the law in Singapore.

Q **Is it illegal to be drunk in a pub in the UK?**

A Indeed it is, according to a law passed in 1872, although these days you would be unlikely to be arrested for it unless you are causing a nuisance or posing a danger to yourself or someone else.

The only way you can get legally blotto is in a private place (i.e. your home or somebody else's), provided that you are not responsible for a child under seven at the time.

For anybody who has ever been drunk and crawling around the floor at four in the morning, the reasons why drunken people should not be in charge of small children should be clear.

Q **Why is it illegal to fill up your own car with petrol in some states of the US?**

A Yes, you read that right. In two states in America – New Jersey and Oregon, to be exact – it is illegal to  get out of your car at a petrol station and fill up your own tank with fuel. The stations in these states are manned and a paid attendant will come out and 'pump your gas' (as they say in the US) for you. There are various arguments for why this is the case. It is claimed that having attendants lowers the insurance cost of a petrol station, thus reducing the price of fuel. It is also said that the practice helps the job market by providing more employment to the population. Whether these are really good enough reasons to make it a law or not, New Jersey and Oregon are sticking to it, and fully enforcing it.

Q Why must a moving car always have its headlights on in Denmark?

A To distinguish it from parked cars, any vehicle in operation in Denmark must always have its headlights on at any time of day. This may sound a bit silly, as it surely can't be that hard to tell the difference between a moving or stationary vehicle – a lack of a driver is usually a bit of a clue – however, since the introduction of this law more than 25 years ago, traffic accidents in the country have significantly decreased.

Q Are high-heeled shoes really illegal in Alabama?

A They are indeed, due to a court case where a woman who caught the heel of her shoe in a grating on the pavement sued the council as she had fallen over and injured herself. After she won her case the city quickly passed the law, stating, 'it is unlawful to wear women's pumps with sharp, high heels'.

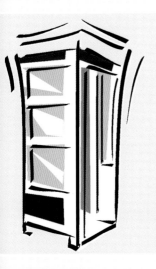

Q Where in America is it 'mandatory for a motorist with criminal intentions to stop at the city limits and telephone the chief of police as he is entering the town'?

A Believe it or not, this is the actual wording of a Washington state law, set up to try and stem the rapidly increasing crime rate in the area. Obviously, due to its sheer stupidity, it has not changed a thing.

Q **Why are couches not permitted on outside porches in Boulder, Colorado?**

A This rather strange-sounding city law stems from the wild partying ways of the students at the University of

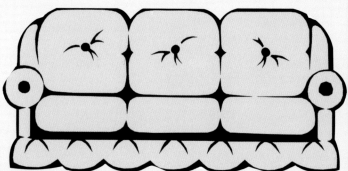

Colorado in Boulder. The university is so infamous it was voted number one party school in America in the 2003 edition of the *Princeton Review*. A common practice after winning a big American football game or following an exam was for the students to burn couches. To prevent this potentially dangerous activity, the law was passed. Essentially it says, 'if you don't want students to burn your stuff, don't leave it where they can get at it'.

Q **Why were mince pies once banned in the UK?**

A During the 1640s, the English parliament banned the eating of mince pies on Christmas day, saying that they were 'insufficiently puritan'. Ingredients of mince pies were pagan in origin, and so they were banned along with other things pagan in origin – such as plum pudding, dancing in church, holly and ivy decorations and maypoles. The law banning these things was never repealed as, when the monarchy was restored and Charles II took the throne, all laws formed under Cromwell were ignored as invalid.

Q Could you go to prison in Arizona for refusing someone a glass of water?

A Well, maybe not prison, but you could be due for a hefty fine. It is illegal in the state of Arizona to refuse someone a glass of water due to the ridiculously hot summers they have there, often reaching temperatures of 120°. Mainly aimed at the homeless, who cannot afford to go into shops and buy water, this law was passed so that businesses were obliged to hand out tap water for free. Convenience stores are the main businesses that uphold this law.

Q What law governs the watering of plants in Cottage Grove, Minnesota?

A The rather complicated-sounding law reads as follows: 'Residents of even-numbered addresses may not water their plants on odd-numbered days, excluding the 31st day where it applies.' Presumably the same law in reverse was true of residents of odd-numbered houses. This law was passed in an admirable effort to save water. However, as it was not specified how much water could be used, there was nothing to stop people watering their plants twice as much half as often, and therefore using exactly the same amount of water as before.

Q What are the London Hackney Carriage laws?

A Covering taxis in London and other towns throughout the UK, the Hackney Carriage laws were set up more than 100 years ago and remained unchanged for quite some time. What caused them to be repealed was protests and industrial action in the Seventies, when drivers demanded that certain laws be upheld – just to annoy the council – such as the one that read 'London Hackney Carriages must carry a bale of hay and a sack of oats' (obviously from the days when cabs were drawn by horses). The council was also obliged to provide a water trough at taxi ranks, where the cabs were to be tethered. These laws were repealed in 1976.

Q When is it legal for a man to urinate in public in the UK?

A When he does so 'on the rear wheel of his motor vehicle' as long as 'his right hand is on the vehicle', according to the century-old Hackney Carriage Laws.

Q Are camels protected by law in Arizona?

A This is a commonly cited law, and at one time, because the US Army and Western entrepreneurs imported camels to the Arizona desert, there may well have been a law protecting them from being hunted. However, no such law exists now.

Q Why can you not step on the currency in Thailand?

A Well, you could, but to be caught doing so would lead to a jail sentence and – quite often – a severe beating. This is because all the bills and coins in Thailand feature a picture of the king, who is held in very high esteem there. To step on the currency is to tread on the king's likeness and therefore would demonstrate a lack of respect.

Q Why are skunks banned from Tennessee?

A Technically the smelly creatures are not banned from the state, however it is illegal to bring one into the state due to the fact that skunks are notorious carriers of rabies. The law was passed to prevent the disease entering Tennessee. Not to mention the smell.

Q Why is there a law limiting the amount of toilets a building has in Waldron Island, Washington?

A The text of said law reads as follows: 'No structure shall contain more than two toilets that use potable water for flushing.' As with many islands, water conservation is a major concern, and this law was obviously set up with that in mind. However, the authorities failed to realise that people will need to go to the toilet regardless of how many toilets there actually are, so the same amount of water is always going to get used.

Q What 'wild west' law is still around today?

A In the city of Austin in the state of Texas it is still illegal to carry wire-cutters in your pocket. This dates back to the time of the 'wild west' when cowboys would cut through the barbed wire fences put up by farmers and property owners, and allow their cattle herds to pass through, trampling the farmers' land. While this is no longer a problem, the law still stands as a salute to Austin's 'wild' past.

Q **Where is 'longbow practice' mandatory by law?**

A In the United Kingdom. The law reads: 'All English males over the age of 14 are to carry out two hours or so of longbow practice a week, supervised by the local clergy'. The law stems from the Middle Ages, when England had no standing army, and each gentry provided a quota of men in times of war. The church was used to regulate things, as it was really the only centralised instrument of bureaucracy around at the time.

Q **Why do you need a permit to beg on the streets of downtown Memphis?**

A A major tourist area, downtown Memphis used to have a problem with numerous and aggressive beggars. To solve the problem, a law was passed stating 'panhandlers must first obtain a permit before begging on the streets of downtown Memphis'. This gave the police more leverage in dealing with the aggressive panhandlers that were driving away tourists and costing the city money.

Q Is it illegal to impersonate a pensioner in the UK?

A Indeed it is, but not just any pensioner, the law states: 'Chelsea pensioners may not be impersonated'. This is because Chelsea pensioners are entitled to enhanced state benefits and cheaper accommodation. Therefore, imitating one would be an act of fraud.

Q Was there once a limit on how many women could live together in Maricopa County, Arizona?

A Yes there was. The law – now repealed – stated, 'no more than six girls may live in any one house'. This law presumably excluded large families, as its purpose in Maricopa County – and many other American towns that also adopted the law – was designed to prevent the proliferation of brothels. However, the law was repealed when sorority houses and university residence halls became commonplace.

Q Is chewing gum illegal in Singapore?

A Sort of. What is actually illegal is the sale of chewing gum. This came about due to the sheer amount of gum that people were dropping and sticking in places such as their underground stations. The practice of chewing the gum is not illegal, just the sale. However, if you are caught placing your chewed gum anywhere other than a bin, you will be slapped with a hefty fine.

Q Why is it illegal to feed deer in the city of Wells in Maine?

A In the interest of public health, plant preservation, traffic control and for their own good, according to the official explanation, which goes as follows: 'The large number of deer attracted by feeding and baiting in and around public and private property increases the local deer population. Deer carry the deer tick known to cause Lyme disease, which is a serious debilitating illness that threatens the public health… In addition, overpopulation and domestication of deer contribute to traffic safety problems and the destruction of important plants and vegetation on public and private property. When deer come to depend on humans for food, the natural order and balance in nature are upset and it is harmful to their long-term well being.'

Q When are horses and 'wheeled transport' banned from Mexico City?

A The animal and the cart he pulls are not welcome in the city during Holy Week, a week of religious festivals that took place throughout the 19th century. The streets would be packed with revellers and so – to avoid trouble – horses and carts were banned from the streets. Another law concerning Holy Week was that fireworks were not to be thrown by hand during this time. Again, this is because of the extremely crowded conditions within the city, and the potentially huge damage a thrown firework could do. These laws were made by Colonel Miguel Maria de Azcarate with the intention of 'preserving the holiness of Holy Week'.

Q Why is the burning of dolls illegal in Mexico?

A This law dates back to colonial Mexico, where people would burn effigies of Judas in imitation of the Inquisition burnings of dead heretics in effigy. By the 1800s these burnings took place as part of a riotous carnival, and the Judas figures were replaced by effigies of powerful leaders in Mexican society that the crowds wanted to poke fun at. By the mid-19th century the celebrations had become so riotous that politicians stepped in and passed the law 'no dolls can be burned that resemble prominent personalities' in the hope of calming things down.

Q What West Virginia law concerns a child's smelly breath?

A The one that reads: 'No child may attend school with their breath smelling of wild onions.' These 'wild onions' of West Virginia are also known as 'ramps' and they are known for their foul aroma which – it is said – can be smelt over a mile away when they are being cooked. Why anyone would eat something that smelled so awful is questionable, however, presumably it was once so much of a problem that, rather than simply pass a school rule about it, the 'smelly breath ban' was made into a state law.

Q **What law connects birds' droppings to land possession in America?**

A The law states: 'A US citizen can take possession of any foreign, uninhabited island, as long as it contains birds' droppings'. This was because guano was once used as a fertilizer for farmers, and was therefore valuable. Islands that were possessed under this law include Midway Island, Christmas Island, Howard Island, Baker Island and Jarvis Island.

Q **Under what circumstances is murder legal in Hong Kong?**

A Wronged women everywhere will be cheering at this one – it is legal for a betrayed wife to kill her adulterous husband in Hong Kong, provided that she do so with her bare hands. However, should she be itching to take someone down with a knife or a pistol, she will be happy to hear that it is also legal for her to kill her husband's mistress any way she pleases.

Q **Why is it illegal for cyclists to remove their feet from the pedals in Mexico?**

A This Mexico City law reads: 'Bicycle riders may not lift either foot from the pedals, as it might result in a loss of control. Also, anyone who whistles at or annoys a bicycle rider could be arrested.' What a thing to go to prison for! The reason behind this outpouring of protection for the cyclist stems from a hit-and-run accident way back in 1895, where a cyclist was killed. Cries went up for the protection of bicycle riders, and the laws were passed.

Q Why is it illegal to picket a funeral in Overland Park, Kansas?

A Or, more importantly, who would want to? This seemingly rather ridiculous law was passed for a very good reason. In Overland Park an individual by the name of Fred Phelps was causing considerable distress to grieving families and friends when he would picket the funerals of known homosexuals in the area. He would yell and scream about what an abomination homosexuality is and about the evil Aids virus sent to rid the world of homosexuals. The police arrested him for disturbing the peace, but other than that there was little they could do, so this law was passed making what he was doing illegal. So far, this seems to have kept Phelps away from the funerals and stopped any other individuals or groups from making their own statements.

Q What is illegal to throw at a parade float in New Orleans, Louisiana?

A A bottle of Coke, apparently. However, although the law reads 'no one may throw a bottle of Coke at a parade float', it is later explained that the law is actually banning the crowd from throwing anything at the parade floats. This may seem unfair, as the people aboard the floats frequently throw things at the crowd. The reasoning is that the crowd expect to be targeted, whereas those on the float could be caught by surprise. Also, they have a lot further to fall!

Q **What law protects the delicate ladies of Alabama?**

A During the civil war, when there was a high military presence in the city, a law was passed making it illegal to 'howl at ladies within the city limits'. This was because the hoots from the soldiers would embarrass the fair maidens. Presumably though, once they were out of city limits, the young ladies did not embarrass quite so easily.

Q **Why is silly string banned in Southington, Connecticut?**

A It's all because of those pesky kids. In the mid-Nineties, a group of children got a little carried away at the Apple Harvest Festival and sprayed a police officer with silly string. The law was passed to stop this from happening again, although – as crimes go – this one does not seem particularly heinous.

Q **What law used to protect prisoners in Alberta, Canada?**

A It used to be law in Alberta that, upon release from prison, any man was given a handgun with bullets and a horse so they could ride out of town. As many of those in prison at the time were there because of gun-related crimes, this law was seldom put into practice and was eventually revoked.

Q In what European countries is it illegal to wear a mask?

A In both Denmark and Germany there is a law in place preventing people from wearing masks. This is in case of a riot or protest, police will be able to see and arrest people more easily if they are not disguised. Presumably it also applies to the other famous mask wearers, such as bank robbers and… erm… superheroes?

Q Why is alcohol banned on certain days in Norway?

A On Election Day in Norway in the early 1900s many workers were intoxicated and therefore their judgement was not what it should be. This was considered such a danger to the democratic process that the sale of 'beverages containing more than 4.75% alcohol' was banned on that day to make sure that voters had a clear mind and knew exactly who they were voting for and why.

Q What law in Swaziland is intended to stop women wearing trousers?

A Since assuming the throne of Swaziland in 2002, King Mswati III has passed several laws with the intention of reforming his country and re-establishing traditional values. Sadly these 'traditional values' seem to hold little in them for the fairer sex as two of the shocking laws that have been passed so far demonstrate. They are: 'Any woman who wears pants faces a possible punishment of having the pants ripped off her and torn to pieces by soldiers' and 'young girls may not shake hands with men'.

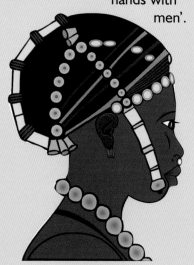

Q Why are meetings held in North Carolina not allowed to be held if members are in costume?

A What at first seems a slightly foolish-sounding law that would make amateur theatre groups uncomfortable actually has a much more sinister reasoning behind it. The Ku Klux Klan were known for wearing their white hooded robes during meetings and demonstrations, both to inflict fear into others while at the same time remaining anonymous. By making these actions illegal, the state hoped to weaken the power of the Ku Klux Klan and drive them out of the state.

Q Why are advertising billboards banned in Hawaii?

A Advertising billboards, or indeed billboards of any nature, are banned from Hawaii under a building code designed to preserve the natural beauty of the views of beaches, volcanoes and mountains. One of the main sources of income in Hawaii is tourism, and therefore the views are not just lovely to look at but, for many of the islanders, represent their livelihood as well.

Q Why must all men wear trousers in Mexico?

A Around the 1890s, members of the Mexican upper classes were anxious to prove to other Western nations that they were as sophisticated and modern as everyone else. With the firm belief that clothes do indeed make the man, they passed the following law: 'All males must wear trousers, and such groups of employees as hack drivers and newspaper delivery boys must adopt uniforms.'

Q Is having more than one child against the law in China?

A It is indeed, although there are a great number of myths about this law and conjecture as to what happens when it is broken. China is the world's most over-populated nation and this law is the government's attempt to exert some control over the situation and hopefully decrease the growth in population. However, the idea that some Westerners have that the Chinese government kills second-borns is entirely false. Rather, there is a large tax for families who have more than one child.

Q Why is there is extra charge put on plastic bottles in Denmark?

A Those clever Danes have come up with an ingenious way to get their nation recycling their plastic bottles. A fee is added on for each bottle at the point of purchase by law. However, a person can claim this money back when they take their bottles to be recycled. So far this scheme has proven extremely successful.

Q

People & Nature

The natural world has many oddities, and the human body provides plenty more – leaving the average person with many unanswered questions. Here we try to answer just a few of those queries regarding the miracles of nature, the wonders of the human body, and the achievements and failings of certain individuals. So, if you've ever wondered how long you could survive without food, or why the sky is blue, then this section has the answers. Also, you can find answers to fascinating questions such as, who invented the paperclip? What are the Seven Wonders of the World? And, why do we get hiccups?

Q Why are normal clouds white but rain clouds black when water is colourless?

A The relative whiteness or darkness of a cloud is a function of cloud depth. The small, puffy white cumuliform clouds that form on sultry summer days shine brightly because the sun reflects off the water droplets. As clouds become bigger and coalesce, light cannot reach the bottom of the cloud and is instead reflected off the top. The vertical extent of the cloud influences the darkness we see from the Earth's surface. The darkest cloud formations occur during thunderstorms, where clouds can sometimes be 20,000 to 30,000 feet high!

Q Can you die laughing?

A Possibly, yes. According to researcher Joost Meerloo, epidemics of laughing, a type of mass hysteria, have been noted since the Middle Ages, and similar episodes are occasionally reported in medical literature today. For instance, it was reported that 1,000 people in Tanganyika suffered a mass laughing fit lasting several days in 1963.

Most of the victims of laughing fits recover. But some die from a combination of starvation and exhaustion. You can't eat or sleep while laughing, and we all know if you try to drink it just sprays out your nose.

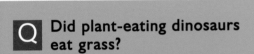

Q **What is the world's most popular fruit?**

A Although many people do not realise it is a fruit, the most popular fruit in the world is the tomato, with more than 60 trillion tons produced per year – 16 million tons more than the banana, which is in second place. Apples are third with 36 million tons, then oranges (34 millions tons) and watermelons (22 million tons).

Q **Did plant-eating dinosaurs eat grass?**

A Scientists think this is unlikely, as they do not believe that grass existed on earth at this time. The landscape during the Mesozoic Era – when dinosaurs lived – was mainly conifers, including trees we have today such as yews, pines, palms, redwoods and the monkey puzzle tree. Flowering plants and grass are thought to have developed many years later.

Q **Who invented Monopoly?**

A A man called Charles Darrow obtained a patent on the game by fraudulently claiming to have drawn up the idea for Monopoly in 1933. He sold the rights two years later to George Parker, the inventor of such games as Risk and Cluedo. However, it later transpired that he had stolen the idea from earlier versions of the game, which were already in existence.

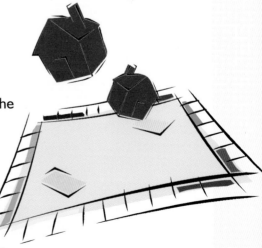

Q How old is the Loch Ness Monster?

A Viking Adamnan wrote the first account of the Loch Ness monster back in 565AD. He told the tale of St Columbia who rowed into the centre of Loch Ness to tell the monster to stop attacking men. Since that time, they say, Nessie has not killed another soul. But sightings of her are still happening – there were five in 1933 alone and the most recent was in 2002. Doctor Kenneth Wilson took the most famous picture of the Loch Ness Monster in 1934. Although the doctor swore the picture was genuine right up to his death in 2001, that same year his friend who was with him at the time the picture was taken revealed that it was a fake. Nessie is also protected by the 1912 Protection of Animals Acts of Scotland – which is not so surprising when you consider she is worth about £20 million annually to the Scottish tourism industry.

Q What was the first animal in space?

A A husky called Laika was the first animal in space, launched by the Soviet Union in 1957. She was followed by two American mice, Laska and Benjy, in 1958, a French cat, Filiette, in 1963 and an American chimpanzee called Ham in 1969.

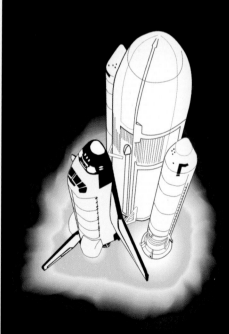

Q Which Ancient Greeks were way ahead of their time?

A Mathematician Pythagoras said that the earth was round way back in the 6th century BC. No one believed him. Nor did they believe astronomer Aristarchos in the 3rd century BC when he said that the earth revolved around the sun. Another man ahead of his time was 2nd century BC astronomer Erastosthenes, who correctly estimated the distance around the earth at about 24,860 miles, but was believed by no one. Sadly they all chose to believe Ptolemy who stated, again in the 2nd century BC, that the earth was the centre of the universe. Most people believed him for the next 1,600 years.

Q Who invented printing?

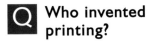

A Although Johannes Gutenberg is widely acknowledged as the inventor of the printing press in 1454, he did not actually invent either printing or moveable type. In 1040 the Chinese used moveable type but discarded the method later, before this they used blocks to print. The oldest surviving printed book is the Buddhist Diamond-Sutra of 868AD. However, Gutenberg was unaware of Chinese printing methods when his experiments revolutionised printing in the Western world. Although an argument with his partners left him financially ruined, Gutenberg remains the most famous printer of all time.

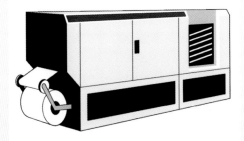

Q Who discovered tea?

A It is said that tea was discovered in China back in 2737BC by an emperor. A breeze was said to have blown some tea leaves into a pot of boiling water and the result was a surprisingly tasty drink. The first European to come into contact with the drink was Jasper de Cruz of Portugal in 1560. The tea bag came into being in 1908 after being invented by Thomas Sullivan of New York.

Q How much iron is there in the human body?

A The average human body contains enough iron to make a 3in nail. But that is not all. It would also contain enough water to fill a 10-gallon tank, enough sulphur to kill all fleas on an average dog, enough potassium to fire a toy cannon, enough fat to make seven bars of soap, enough phosphorous to make 2,200 match-heads, and enough carbon to make 900 pencils.

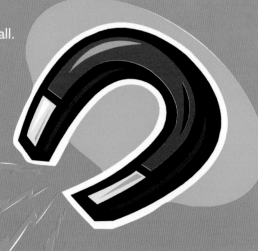

Q How many computers did the chairman of IBM think the world would need back in 1943?

A Thomas Watson is said to have gone on record back in 1943 as saying the world needed 'maybe only five computers'. While there is no concrete evidence that he actually said this, and the earliest source for it is from 1986, it is now widely cited. It is amazing to think that IBM launched the first personal computer in 1981 and now many homes have more than one, not to mention offices, universities and schools...

Q Is Mount Everest still growing?

A According to *National Geographic*, Mount Everest grows about 4mm a year as the tectonic plates of Asia and India – the Eurasian plate and the Indo-Australian plate, which collided millions of years ago to form the Himalayas – continue to press against each other. This causes the Himalayan peaks to grow slightly each year. So not only are the Himalayas the world's tallest mountains, but they are also the fastest growing.

Q How many bones are in a human head?

A There are 22 bones in total that make up the human head, including the cranium and facial bones. The cranium is made up of eight bones – the frontal bone, two parietal bones, two temporal bones, the occipital bone in the back, the ethmoid bone behind the nose, and the sphenoid bone. The face consists of 14 bones including the upper and lower jaw.

Q Why is the sky blue?

A When sunlight travels through the atmosphere, it collides with gas molecules. These molecules scatter the light. The shorter the wavelength of light, the more it is scattered by the atmosphere. Because it has a shorter wavelength than the other colours, blue light is scattered 10 times more than red light, for instance. However, when the sun is on the horizon, its light takes a longer path through the atmosphere to reach your eyes than when the sun is directly overhead. By the time the light of the setting sun reaches your eyes, most of the blue light has been scattered out. The light you finally see is reddish orange, the colour of white light minus blue.

Q What was the initial reaction to the invention of the telephone?

A It is safe to say that the telephone was not widely appreciated in the first 15 years after its invention. Western Union believed their telegraph was superior, and an internal memo, dated 1876, reads: 'This telephone has too many shortcomings to be seriously considered as a means of communication.' When Alexander Graham Bell asked Mark Twain for an investment of $5,000, Twain declined, saying he saw no future in it. But perhaps the best response is that of the British parliament, who saw no need for telephones as 'we have enough messengers here'.

Q When was the last execution in the Tower of London?

A On August 14, 1941, German spy Josef Jakobs was shot by a firing squad at the Tower of London. Because he had suffered a broken ankle when he parachuted into England on January 31, 1941, he could not stand before the firing squad and he was, instead, seated in an old Windsor chair and tied up. Five of the eight shots pierced his heart.

Q What are the Seven Wonders of the World?

A Of the original seven, the only wonder still standing is the Great Pyramid at Giza, built for Pharaoh Khufu. The others – now lost to us – are: the Hanging Gardens of Babylon, built by King Nebuchadnezzar II on the banks of the Euphrates; the gold statue of Zeus at Olympia, built by sculptor Pheidias; the lighthouse of Alexandria, built by the Sostratus of Cnidus on the island of Pharos; the temple of Artemis, in the Asia Minor city of Ephesus, built for the goddess of hunting; the Colossus of Rhodes, built for the sun-god; and the mausoleum at Halicarnassus, a tomb built for King Maussollos, Persian satrap of Caria.

Q Who wrote the first English dictionary?

A Samuel Johnson wrote the first English dictionary in 1755. The first *Oxford English Dictionary* was published in 1928, 50 years after work on it had begun. It had 400,000 words and phrases and was bound in 10 volumes. The most recent edition has 22,000 pages, contains 33,000 Shakespeare quotations and is bound in 20 volumes. Now the whole thing is available on one CD.

Q Who has written the most novels?

A Dame Barbara Cartland is the woman responsible for a staggering 723 novels, which have been translated into 36 languages. Having sold more than 1 billion copies, she is also the biggest-selling novelist of all time.

Q What muscle in the human body moves the fastest?

A The muscle that lets your eye blink is the fastest moving muscle in the body. On average a man will blink 15,000 times a day, and a woman will blink twice as much.

Q Who predicted that radio had no future?

A Back in 1894, the president of the Royal Society predicted that radio had no future. Five years after Lord Kelvin's announcement, the first radio factory opened. And that was not Lord Kelvin's only error. He also stated that flying machines that were heavier than air were impossible. Today there are more than 1 billion radio sets tuned to more than 33,000 radio stations and commercial airline travel is more popular than ever.

Q Who invented the paperclip?

A By the time Johann Vaaler – from Aurskog, Norway – patented his design for a paperclip in 1901, there were also two other similar designs on the books. Cornelius Brosnan of Springfield, Massachusetts, patented his design, called a Konaclip, in 1900, while William Middlebrook of Waterbury, Connecticut, patented his design in 1899. However, it is thought that the credit should really go to Vaaler, as some of his sketches are shown to date back to 1899. However, as Norway had no patent law, he had to seek patent rights in Germany and the US later on.

Q Who was the second man on the moon?

A While everyone knows that Neil Armstrong was the first man on the moon on July 20, 1969, fewer people know that it was Edwin 'Buzz' Aldrin that followed him, and did a lot of the filming. A third member of the Apollo 11 crew, Michael Collins, stayed onboard the mother ship, Columbia. The Apollo 11 plaque left on the moon reads: 'Here men from the planet Earth first set foot upon the moon July 1969, AD. We came in peace for all mankind.'

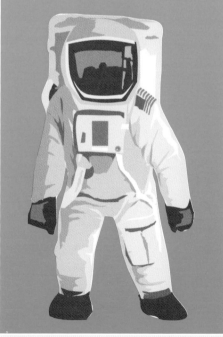

Q Why do we get hiccups?

A Hiccups are caused when the muscle that controls our breathing, the diaphragm, becomes irritated and begins to spasm and contract out of control. Air is pulled into the lungs quickly, passes through the voice box, and then the epiglottis closes behind the rush of air, shaking the vocal chords, causing the hiccup sound. On average, hiccups last for about 5 minutes, and the best way to get rid of them is to breathe into a paper bag, as this calms the diaphragm by increasing the amount of carbon dioxide in your bloodstream.

Q How long can you hold your breath for?

A The average person can hold their breath for one minute. However, the world record is an amazing $7\frac{1}{2}$ minutes! You breathe, on average, about 23,000 times a day.

Q Further Funnies

Some of the best and most intriguing questions are found in this amusing miscellaneous section. Containing tricky queries concerning such varying subjects as inventions, dates, food, and art, this is a good section to randomly dip in and out of. So, if you've ever wondered why we celebrate Valentine's Day on February 14th, or why we play practical jokes on April 1st, then look no further. Also, you can discover how long the 100-Years War lasted (not as easy a question as you may think) and why onions make you cry.

Q Why do we drive on the left in England, when the rest of the world drives on the right?

A This is a bit of trick question, as over 50 countries drive on the left, including Commonwealth countries such as Australia, New Zealand, Pakistan and Jamaica, but also Japan and Indonesia. The custom is thought to have originated in England during the Middle Ages, when life was more dangerous; as most people were right-handed, they rode on the left of the road to leave their sword arms free in case of any trouble. Napoleon ordered the French to travel on the right, as this was the traditional side for the French peasantry during the monarchy; this law was extended to all territories conquered by him.

Q What brought about the broadsheet paper?

A This is said to be due to the 1712 imposition in Britain of a newspaper tax, based on the number of pages in the paper. Publishers therefore doubled the size and halved the number of pages in order to pay less tax, giving us the modern broadsheet format, although this is currently being phased out by most national papers.

(Similarly, a tax imposed in Holland, based on the width of the frontage of houses, is responsible for the famously narrow houses of Amsterdam.)

Q Why do we play
practical jokes on April 1st?

A It is thought that the origin of April Fools' Day was in the 1500s
when the Julian calendar was taken oven by the Gregorian
calendar. The New Year had previously been celebrated on April 1st, and
so those who could be tricked into celebrating it
then were known as 'April fools'. However, this
is only one theory. *The Encyclopaedia
Britannica* suggests, 'The timing of this day
of pranks seems to be related to the arrival
of spring, when nature 'fools' mankind with
fickle weather'. However it began, it has
since evolved its own superstitions and
folklore, such as pranks must be played
before noon, otherwise bad luck will
curse the prankster.

Q Why do we celebrate
Valentine's Day on February 14th?

A Originally the day was celebrated on February
15th in honour of the Roman gods Lupercus and
Faunus. It was called the fertility festival of Lupercalia,
and young men would draw the names of women from a
box and each couple would be paired until the next year's celebration. Often the couples would fall in love and marry. When Rome
was facing battles and civil unrest in 270AD Emperor Claudius II can-
celled all engagements and weddings in order to get men to sign up for
battle. Two priests continued to perform wedding ceremonies
illegally, Valentine and Marius. Valentine was caught and thrown in
prison on February 14th. He was later beheaded. Made the lover's saint,
Valentine's Day was then a Roman Catholic celebration until it was
removed from the religious calendar in 1969.

Q **What is the smallest island in the world?**

A According to the *Guinness Book of Records* it is Bishop Rock, which lies south west of England. It is one of 1040 islands around Britain and has only a lighthouse on it. According to the 1861 guidelines for defining an island, if it is inhabited then size is irrelevant, but if it is uninhabited then it had to be 'the summer's pasturage of at least one sheep' before being classed as an island. This equates to roughly two acres.

Q **When was the first email sent?**

A A man called Ray Tomlinson sent the first email in 1972. He was also the man behind the idea of using the @ sign to separate the name of the user from the name of the computer.

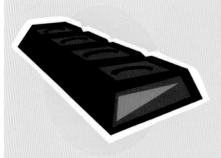

Q **What nation eats the most chocolate?**

A Rather appropriately it is the Swiss that consume the largest amount of chocolate per person, at an average of 10kg each, compared to America's unimpressive 5kg.

Q What came first, traffic lights or the motorcar?

A Traffic lights were used before the invention of the motorcar. In 1868 a lantern was used with red and green signals at a London intersection to control the flow of horse-pulled buggies and pedestrians. They were also used as railroad signals, which were adapted by adding an amber light to be used for cars. Officer William Potts introduced manually controlled electric traffic lights in Detroit, Michigan in 1920. The first automatic traffic lights were used in Cleveland, Ohio, after being invented later in 1920 by Garrett Morgan.

Q What is the largest aircraft ever built?

A Eccentric millionaire Howard Hughes commissioned the building of the Spruce Goose in the 1940s and it flew in November 1947 for one mile at an altitude of 70ft. Built as a prototype transport for troops, the plane weighed in at 140 tons and had a wingspan on 320ft. When the Pentagon rejected it, Hughes put the plane into storage and it was never flown again. Although he was taken to court for war profiteering, Hughes walked away an innocent man. At that time, his eccentricities were out of control and he lived the remainder of his life, until his death in 1976, as a recluse.

Q When did petrol cars replace electric cars?

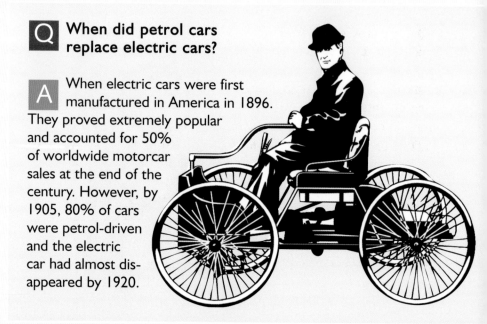

A When electric cars were first manufactured in America in 1896. They proved extremely popular and accounted for 50% of worldwide motorcar sales at the end of the century. However, by 1905, 80% of cars were petrol-driven and the electric car had almost disappeared by 1920.

Q Who invented the first vending machine?

A Hero of Alexandria invented the first coin-operated vending machine around 15BC to dispense water. A coin was placed in a slot, the weight of which would pull a cork out and dispense a trickle of water.

Q What happened between September 3rd and 13th, 1752?

A Absolutely nothing! No one was born, no one died and no one did anything, simply because these days did not exist. This was the time the Julian calendar was replaced by the Gregorian calendar in Britain and the American colonies. As the Julian calendar was 11 days behind the Gregorian, September 14th followed September 2nd.

Q Did Coca-Cola really once contain cocaine?

A Yes it did! It was named in 1885 after its two 'medicinal' ingredients – coca leaves and kola nuts. Back in 1885 cocaine was considered a medicine and used in many patent medicines. It is hard to say exactly how much coca leaf was in the original formula, but it was an extremely small amount. It is said that cocaine continued to be an ingredient after people started to question its use, in order to protect their trade name. By 1902 Coca-Cola contained as little as 1/400 of a grain of cocaine per ounce of syrup. This amount continued to diminish until the completely cocaine-free version of the drink was marketed in 1929.

Q Why do hamburgers contain no ham?

A A hamburger should be made up of 70–80% beef as well as fat and spices. It is thought that a German merchant took a trip to Asia in the early 1800s and noticed that the nomadic Tartars kept their meat under their saddles to soften it. The meat was pounded to bits, and then scraped back together and seasoned for consumption. He took this idea back to his hometown of Hamburg and it caught on. When German immigrants arrived in America, they brought the recipe with them, known as 'Hamburg meat'. It is said the term 'hamburger' originally appeared on the menu of New York's Delmonico's restaurant in 1834, but there is no existing proof. In 1885 the hamburger as we know it appeared, but there are two claims to being its creator. It was either Charlie Nagreen or Frank and Charles Menches who arrived at a New York county fair to prepare their famous pork meat sandwiches, only to find the local butcher had no pork and so they used what was available – beef.

Q **Why do golf courses have 18 holes?**

A There is a delightful story about this that says that one of the members of St Andrews golf club in 1858 pointed out that it takes exactly 18 holes to polish off a fifth of a bottle of Scotch, providing he allowed himself one shot per hole. Therefore a game of golf was finished when the Scotch ran out. Sadly, this is just a story. St Andrews originally had 22 holes – 11 fairways played both ways. In 1764 two of the fairways were considered too short and attached to the others to make nine fairways and 18 holes. The original rulebook, drawn up by the Royal and Ancient Golf Club of St Andrews, used this as the standard, and soon 18 holes became the norm.

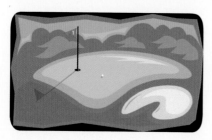

Q **Why is blue the favoured colour for boys?**

A Back in ancient times, evil spirits were thought to linger over nurseries, hoping to take the souls of the young. To combat these spirits, parents would dress little boys – who back then were more precious than baby girls – in blue, the colour most associated with the heavenly spirits. Girls would mainly be clothed in black. Pink for girls came about in the Middle Ages, but the origins of the colour choice are not clear.

Q How long did the 100-Years War last?

A The war between Britain and France – the longest war in history – actually lasted 116 years, before coming to an end in 1453. During this time income tax was introduced in Britain as a way of funding the feud with the French. The shortest war in history happened in 1896. Zanzibar surrendered to Britain after exactly 38 minutes.

Q Why do onions make you cry?

A Onions, like other plants, are made of cells. The cells are divided into two sections separated by a membrane. One side of the membrane contains an enzyme, which helps chemical processes occur in your body. The other side of the membrane contains molecules that contain sulphur. When you cut an onion, the contents on each side of the membrane mix and cause a chemical reaction. This reaction produces molecules such as ethylsufine which make your eyes water. Cutting an onion under running water, or putting it in the freezer before cutting it are both effective ways of preventing the eye watering.

Q Has the Mona Lisa ever been stolen?

A Yes, back in 1912 Leonardo da Vinci's masterpiece was stolen from the Louvre in Paris. Six replicas were sold at huge prices, claiming to be the original, before the true original was discovered three years later and returned to the Louvre, where it still hangs today.

Q How were tins opened before the tin opener was invented?

A Peter Durand of London invented the tin canister in 1810. Tinned food became popular around 1846 when a machine was invented to speed up production. Labels on tins read: 'Cut around on top, near to outer edge with a chisel and hammer.' The tin opener was invented by American Ezra Warnet in 1858 but did not become popular until it was given away with canned beef 10 years later. The tin opener as we know it today was invented in 1925.

Q Why does the Leaning Tower of Pisa lean?

A When construction began in 1173, the foundation of the tower settled unevenly and work was abandoned. However, work began again 100 years later using the same foundation and the finished tower leaned visibly towards the south. Regular measuring of the tower began in 1911 and since then the tower has moved 1.2mm each year, meaning that the top of the tower is 5.3m off-centre. Engineers are currently working to stabilise the base of the tower in order to ease the top back, but the tower will still lean.